REMEMBERING PE
RAYMOND BURR

(Includes never-before-published conversations with the legendary actor!)

Brian McFadden

BAILEY *BISHOPS*
PRESS

Kohner, Madison & Danforth

ISBN 13: 978-0-692-63850-7
ISBN: 0-692-63850-4

DEDICATION

This book is dedicated to the late Raymond Burr ... an extremely talented actor who also just happened to be a very nice guy and a great storyteller! Also, to the many "Perry Mason" fans who, like me, always wanted to know more about the classic TV show and the actors who made Erle Stanley Gardner's characters come alive.

And to Pat: My wife, best friend (and favorite editor!)

TABLE OF CONTENTS

Preface vi

(The Case of the)
Tantalizing Time Machine..........................1

(The Case of the)
Aggravated Author 11

(The Case of the)
Triumphant Tryout 23

(The Case of the)
Colorful Co-Stars 31

(The Case of the)
Rose-Colored Glasses 41

(The Case of the)
Bewildering Biographies 55

(The Case of the)
B-Movie Barrister.....................................63

(The Case of the)
Gangbusters vs. Godzilla..........................67

(The Case of the)
Loquacious Locations...............................73

(The Case of the)
Counselor's Comeback 87

(The Case of the)
Fulfilling Finale 91

PREFACE

Have you ever watched a "Perry Mason" re-run and found that "Who Done It" wasn't the only mystery you wanted solved? More than most pioneering programs, it seems, the long-running series inspires otherwise normal, ordinary viewers to ask themselves questions which simply don't come up when watching your typical TV show.

For example, ever find yourself wondering, "Were times really so much simpler years ago?" Or maybe you wish you knew how the cast members got along? What was it like to be on the set and—for that matter—where was "the set?" (As it turns out, there were many different sets and studios, depending on the production year, but more on that later.)

These and so many other questions ran through my mind every time I'd see an old "Perry Mason" episode. Maybe it's because the program somehow seems suspended in time. Perhaps I just want to go back there because I was only a youngster when the programs originally aired.

Whatever the reason, the one thing I *do* know is that I am not alone. Over the years, I've heard from many people who have felt the same way, and the number keeps growing as the series shows up in re-runs on more and more outlets ... everything from video streaming to DVD and cable.

If, like me, you are a victim of what I like to call "The Case of the Compulsively Curious Viewer," I may have some good news for you. As one of those viewers, who grew up to cover the entertainment business, I was fortunate enough to discuss these matters with a man who had an intimate knowledge of all the details. That man, of course, was Raymond Burr. It is my sincere hope that many of the questions I asked the actor all those years ago, are the same ones you always wanted to ask too. If so, this book is for you!

THE CASE OF THE TANTALIZING TIME MACHINE

Tantalize (/'Tan-tal-ize/)—Definition: "To create extreme desire by showing a person something they yearn for which will forever remain unobtainable."

Yes, "Tantalizing" is definitely the word to describe "Perry Mason," a TV program that offers a fascinating glimpse into the fifties and sixties. And, as the definition above suggests, the show can create in many of us an "extreme desire' or "yearning" for the past. But, of course, it's a desire that will "forever remain unobtainable" because we can never really go back there. However, many would argue that the next best thing is the vicarious pleasure we can experience by watching this iconic program.

Some fans of the show are new. Others, like yours truly, grew up with the program and can barely remember a time when Raymond Burr wasn't Perry Mason. He paid a visit to our house every week and he was always a welcomed guest. The show was the one program the entire family could agree on. My brother and I might grumble a bit when my mom and dad wanted to watch a variety show while we wanted to see a western (remember, this was in the days of only one TV) but there was no debate about America's favorite lawyer.

We'd all gather around the TV set and usually my parents would let us have some ice cream, which may be one of the reasons I think of the show as a kind of "comfort food." Then again, it could be because the series was, in some respects, a lot like those mysteries the British refer to as "cozies." Just as a reader can enjoy an Agatha Christie and escape the concerns of everyday life, a viewer can watch "Perry Mason" and be sure good will triumph over evil in the end, without too much sex or violence along the way.

Then there's the pure nostalgia of viewing the cars, the stately buildings, clean streets ... even the different hair styles and women's fashions. (The men's too—did all the guys wear hats back then?)

And, of course, there was the man himself, Perry Mason as portrayed by Raymond Burr.

As a youngster I couldn't really distinguish between the talented and compassionate lawyer I saw every week and the man who played him on the small screen. And it's a pleasure to report that, as an adult, I found out there wasn't really any need to. Raymond Burr the person, shared many of the same positive traits attributed to the fictional attorney he portrayed.

I came into contact with many celebrities over the years, but every once in a while I'd meet someone really special like Raymond Burr. He wasn't just one of the nicest actors I ever met—he was one of the nicest *people* I ever met.

The author and Raymond Burr

Here was a man known around the world, who didn't surround himself with studio representatives or public relations people all the time. That alone set him apart from most celebrities.

Maybe it was because his major success came later in life, or perhaps he was just one of those people who had the ability to connect with others one-on-one, but I remember that he certainly had the knack for making you feel comfortable. Raymond Burr, the TV and movie star, seemed larger-than-life and many of the publicity stories about him turned out to be huge exaggerations or outright falsehoods. But it was impossible not to like the guy in person.

He drew you in with his friendliness and lack of pretension. Burr seemed to be one of those people who never forgot the early days before he found fame. Deep down, he was a hard working actor who paid his dues. He had struggled for years to make it in the business before "Perry Mason" came along.

Young actor Raymond Burr

Things were finally beginning to break Burr's way when the "Mason" role became available. At the time, his relatively recent performance in "Rear Window" was still fresh in the minds of Hollywood casting directors. But Raymond Burr was still far from being a household name. And even after he won the role and waited for the first show to air, the actor told me it was still touch and go.

Because the program became such an iconic show, perhaps—like many fans—you've always assumed "Perry Mason" was smooth sailing from the beginning. I know I did, which is why I was so surprised when Burr told me "Perry Mason" was more a case of going into uncharted waters. In fact, he explained, it was a matter of "cross your fingers and hope for the best."

"You have to remember that, in those days, nobody knew where television was going," the actor explained. I was confused to hear him say that because I always thought the pioneering days of television were in the late forties and very early fifties. But Burr pointed out that everything was still in flux a few years later when the "Mason" show was being planned.

"We were among the first of the hour shows ... the first of the hour-long *drama* shows at any rate," he said. "Don't forget," he added, "we didn't know if it was going to be accepted."

Because "Perry Mason" was on until 1966, it's easy to forget that the show got its start a decade earlier. Although the program didn't go on the air until September of 1957, the pilot was filmed the year before, in the fall of 1956. At the time, half-hour sitcoms and westerns were popular, and so were quiz shows and variety programs.

Live television anthologies were still around and there was even talk early on of "Perry Mason" being shot live, something that thankfully didn't happen. The logistics would have been a nightmare. Burr said it was tough enough shooting an hour-long program on film without falling behind. The fact that much of the second half of the show was confined to the courtroom set helped a little, but it was still difficult to keep on schedule.

Burr told me it took a tremendous effort by all involved to turn out the equivalent of a short movie every six days. "Everybody really worked hard and there was so much dedication," he said. "Not just from the actors, but from the crews, and from the writers and from the producers. Everybody worked very hard and very long. But it wasn't just the hard work, because television, as you know, is always very hard work."

I *did* know that, because I had been on both TV and movie sets. Movies were more like "Hurry up and wait." An actor gets called to the set and then winds up sitting around cooling their heels while technicians fool around with the lighting or someone decides to make script changes. It can be very boring. But with TV, especially if you're doing a series, everybody's racing against the clock ... essentially shooting a film in a little over a week. Somehow it worked with "Mason," but not without a lot of sacrifice.

"That's why I say it was more than just the hard work everybody put in on the show," said Burr. "There was something extra ... an extra bit of dedication."

And Raymond Burr was right at the top of the list when it came to "extra dedication." While the star of any television show generally has the most on-screen time, programs like "Perry Mason" are in a class all their own. Think about it for a minute and you'll immediately realize why.

Each "Mason" show normally had a brief intro in which we were introduced to the characters and the crime. Once that's finished, however, Perry enters stage left and shows up in almost every scene. The fact that the second half of the program takes place in the courtroom, where Perry is the main focus of attention, only added to the necessity of his presence on the set almost all the time.

True, Bill Talman had to be around for most of the second half of the shows too. After all, his role as DA Hamilton Burger demanded that he be in court to lose all those cases week after week.

And, in the early shows, Ray Collins, as Lieutenant Tragg, was right next to him at the prosecution's table. But Talman and Collins were usually present for only a few scenes outside the courtroom.

William Hopper, as Paul Drake, would breeze into Perry's office to deliver a cheery greeting to Della and get instructions from his boss. But he only came to court when he had some late-breaking clue for Perry. For the most part, Hopper moved in and out of the plot, and the number of scenes in which he appeared varied by episode.

Barbara Hale spent a lot of time sitting beside her boss in

the courtroom, but she rarely had many lines in those scenes. On occasion, when Perry sent Della on a mission, Barbara would become involved with the plot, but – for the most part – her main scenes were in the office.

Della in the office

So obviously, while the rigors of a weekly one-hour show were hardly a walk in the park for his co-stars, it was Burr who was required to do most of the heavy lifting.

That's why one thing the various studios that were used to shoot "Perry Mason" had in common was a large dressing room or bungalow that Burr could use so he could stay overnight if necessary, to save commuting time. With the long hours and early-morning calls, Burr would often work all day, grab a little sleep and then be up before dawn to do it all over again. And don't forget, this was in the days of 39 episodes per season.

Although Raymond told me he had little time away from the studio when the show was filming, he didn't seem to have any real regrets. Despite the heavy workload when the show was in production, I have the feeling the perfectionist streak in Burr would have made it difficult for him to do things any other way at that time. Later he expressed some concern that perhaps he had stayed with the original series a little bit too long. But he had wanted the role and was thrilled to get it, even though—unlike the movie Perry Masons before him—he would become forever identified with the character.

THE CASE OF THE AGGRAVATED AUTHOR

As an old mystery movie fan, I asked Raymond Burr about the early Perry Mason films that were released in the thirties. Well-respected actors like Warren William, Ricardo Cortez and Donald Woods had starred in them, but any memories of their performances were totally eclipsed once Burr took over the role.

Movie Mason Warren William

"I think those pictures were done at Warner Brothers and there was nothing wrong with the acting in them," said Burr. "But they were not what Mr. Gardner expected to see or wanted, so he wouldn't allow any more pictures to be made." (Notice that the actor referred to the author as "Mr.

Gardner." He did so every time he mentioned Perry Mason's creator to me, and I presume it's the way he thought of him. Raymond Burr was a world-famous star when he and I were talking, but his reverence for the man who helped him gain that fame never faltered, and he always used the preface "Mr." when referring to Gardner.)

Burr was correct in remembering Warner Brothers as the studio and the main problem was that they were trying to fit the character into the popular detective mold of the day. The studio's first choice as Perry, Warren William, had played "Philo Vance" and the producers seemed to have that popular detective and "The Thin Man" in mind when they set about "fine tuning" Perry for greater box-office appeal.

After his displeasure with the films, Gardner was determined not to lose control of the property again. He took his time setting up a deal for the TV show, making sure that he had the final say on most matters of any importance. And the choice of an actor to play Mason on television was a matter of great importance!

We'll take a closer look at how Burr was actually chosen for the role in the next chapter. But for now, let's consider how unlikely it was that Raymond was even in the running for the role. Remember, up until he auditioned for Perry Mason, Burr was mainly known for his "Bad Guy" background in films. I, for one, was quite impressed by the turnaround. And I wanted to let him know that I thought it was a pretty amazing feat.

"I don't know too many actors who have managed to successfully pull off what you did in mid-career," I said. "You became one of the most popular leading men on TV after years of playing heavies in movies, not an easy thing to do."

Burr agreed that the Mason role was a huge turning point, but said he'd been working on changing his image for quite some time prior to testing for the series.

"I was trying to pull away from doing heavies in early television," he said. "I mean you run out of ways of playing the heavy after a while." Then Burr laughed and added, "You just run out of ways of being killed!"

Burr being menaced by Errol Flynn

Although Burr was of course joking about the difficulties of having to find different ways to die, he definitely wasn't kidding about doing his best to change his movie image in early television. In fact, in the 1951 pilot episode of "Dragnet," the actor plays Jack Webb's boss, Deputy Chief Thad Brown.

The Christian TV program "Family Theater" gave

Raymond some high-profile opportunities to turn around his villainous image too. In 1952's "A Star Shall Rise," he plays a skeptical member of the Three Magi who becomes a believer.

As if playing one of the three wise men wasn't enough, in a 1953 "Family Theater" presentation entitled "The Triumphant Hour," Raymond Burr was actually cast as Saint Peter!

But Burr couldn't seem to shake his reputation as the go-to-guy for heavies among movie producers and studio casting directors. On the big screen he continued to play bad guys, mostly because he was just so darn good at it.

Even in mediocre movies like "Mara Maru" with Errol Flynn and "Bandits of Corsica" with Richard Greene, Burr's performances stand out. It was the same with some of his better pictures too. At the same time he was making progress toward less lethal roles on TV, he was being cast as a sleazy lothario who tries to seduce Ann Baxter in "Blue Gardenia."

Burr was an even more memorable villain in the Alfred Hitchcock classic "Rear Window."

Raymond provided just the right touch of menace to keep audiences on the edge of their seats as they pondered the fate of stars Jimmy Stewart and Grace Kelley. What makes his strong performance all the more remarkable is the fact that, for most of the film, Burr is glimpsed only from a distance.

The list of movies that found him playing bandits, henchmen and psychos continued to grow—"Count Three and Pray" with Van Heflin and "A Man Alone" with Ray Milland, both in 1955, and the stalker melodrama "A Cry in the Night" with his frequent date on publicity outings, Natalie Wood, in 1956.

Raymond scares Natalie: "A Cry in the Night"

Burr said, even though he realized most movie producers couldn't seem to see him playing anything but a heavy, he never really thought of himself that way. But he told me he could understand why so many people thought of him as being "born-to-play-the-bad-guy" right up until he won the part of Perry Mason.

"From motion pictures I suppose you'd have to say I almost always was the villain," he said. "But, prior to that, I actually played very few villains in the theater. In fact, I started out with a musical!"

Now, Raymond Burr in a musical was hard to imagine. So I had to ask him "*What* musical and *When*?

"It was in 1941, I believe. It was called 'Crazy with the Heat,' and I was singing and dancing in it!"

Sure enough, I looked it up and Raymond Burr was indeed in the Broadway Musical Revue "Crazy with the Heat." And, yes, it featured a series of sketches in which our future Perry Mason does, indeed, get a chance to put his dancing and singing talents on display. The only more recent time, he told me, that he had the opportunity to put his crooning abilities to good use was on a TV show he did in Australia.

This was another little factoid that I looked up later. It turned out Burr was referring to a variety show he appeared on in Melbourne during a 1961 Australian trip. (He joked about his singing with me, but I wouldn't be surprised if he wasn't really quite good. After all, just listening to him speak provided plenty of evidence that he had the pipes for it!)

Getting back to his early career, the actor explained that, while "Crazy with the Heat" wasn't a big success, he fared better with a straight dramatic role he landed later.

"I was in a play that Alexander Cohen produced," said Burr. "That was 1943 and it was called "The Duke in

Darkness."

The show itself didn't exactly take Broadway by storm, but Raymond got noticed and it was a definite plus for his career. He certainly cut a dashing figure in the play.

As he appeared in "The Duke in Darkness"

Burr received good reviews for his performance and an agent who saw him in "The Duke in Darkness" helped arrange a contract for him at RKO Studios. It certainly seemed like a promising start and the young actor was optimistic. However, initially, RKO didn't do much with

Raymond. He got a few walk-ons and bit parts, and played a convincing heavy in one or two films, but that was about it. On the plus side, Burr did eventually wind up in "Desperate," an excellent film noir directed by Anthony Mann that was released by RKO in 1947. Even though this is only one of his first films with on-screen credit, many critics feel that he steals the show.

Torment...
Tension...
TERROR!

Guiltless two
... hunted by
hijackers ...
hounded by the
law...ready to kill
for the right to live!

WITH
STEVE BRODIE
AUDREY LONG
RAYMOND BURR · DOUGLAS FOWLEY
WILLIAM CHALLEE · JASON ROBARDS
Produced by MICHEL KRAIKE · Directed by ANTHONY MANN
Screen Play by HARRY ESSEX

Burr's career really gained momentum as a freelancer. He found himself typecast as a villain, but he was getting plenty of work. It's actually rather amazing that he accomplished as much as he did in the late forties. Between 1946 and 1949 he appeared in a total of 18 films. At first the actor was hired mostly at lower echelon studios like Eagle-Lion (the former poverty row outfit PRC,) which distributed Edward Small's

"Raw Deal." The film starred Dennis O'Keefe, Claire Trevor, John Ireland and Marsha Hunt.

Burr with John Ireland and Marsha Hunt

Film noir was gaining popularity at the time and the genre was ideal for Raymond Burr's brand of evil menace. As word spread of Burr's powerful performances in relatively small budget films, he was able to branch out and find work at Paramount and Warner Brothers too. Some of his early roles were small, but others were quite large and provided a real showcase for his talents.

And the actor was even busier in the early fifties than he was in the forties. Even as television was beginning to take hold, the kinds of gritty films that Burr was perfect for continued to draw movie audiences. He delivered a strong performance in RKO's "His Kind of Woman," which featured Robert Mitchum, Jane Russell and Vincent Price.

Brandishing a gun in "His Kind of Woman."

Between 1951's "His Kind of Woman" and his debut as TV's "Perry Mason" in 1957, Burr would make over 30 films. Some were straight westerns, like "Horizons West" with Rock Hudson and Robert Ryan. Others were cavalry oaters like "Thunder Pass" with Dane Clark and Andy Devine.

Burr appeared in a few low-budget desert epics too, including "Fort Algiers" with Yvonne De Carlo. And, not to miss out on the comedy front, Burr showed up in movies like "Casanova's Big Night" with Bob Hope and "You're Never Too Young" with Dean Martin and Jerry Lewis.

The future "Perry Mason" even did an "Arabian Nights" saga called "The Magic Carpet," with the future "Lucy

Ricardo," Lucille Ball.

But Burr is mostly remembered for his film noir appearances during this period in movies like "FBI Girl" with Cesar Romero, George Brent and Audrey Totter.

Baddie Burr with Audrey Totter in "FBI Girl."

I asked Raymond if he had a rough guess as to how many movies he made prior to being chosen for "Perry Mason." He thought for just a moment and then said, "I think, between 1946 and 1956, I did about 90 motion pictures!" That's an awful lot of movies and in most of them he was on the wrong side of the law!

THE CASE OF THE TRIUMPHANT TRYOUT

Over the years I never lost my love for "Perry Mason" and I'd catch re-runs whenever they were on, but the occasions on which a local channel would broadcast old episodes were few and far between. Remember, this was in the days before video tape, let alone DVDs, Netflix and video streaming! There are certainly some bad things about the internet, but there are some wonderful things too. Suddenly, we have historic moments in media history at our fingertips.

While I was writing this book, I had the opportunity to watch a few of those historic moments—the 1956 screen tests of Raymond Burr for the roles of both Perry Mason and his arch-nemesis Hamilton Burger, as well as William Hopper's screen test for Perry Mason. We get to see Burr and Hopper auditioning in scenes that take place both in the office *and* in the courtroom.

Because the actors eventually chosen were so perfect, we tend to think of them as having simply materialized on the set one day without the necessity of tryouts ... a little like Scotty beaming up Captain Kirk! But that was far from the case.

In reality the competition was fierce. There were scores of actors who tested for the role. It had to be a tense time for Burr, but he told me he had one man in his corner that made all the difference.

"When the television possibility came along, I guess they must have tested 100 actors and I was number 101 or 102," he laughed. "And Mr. Gardner (Perry Mason author Erle Stanley Gardner,) decided that I was what he wanted in the show as far as how he thought Perry Mason should look and it went from there. I stayed with it and I enjoyed doing it."

Actually, Burr was being modest. It wasn't just his looks. Even the most cursory glance at those audition reels shows exactly what Gardner must have seen in the tall, commanding actor, whose expressive face added subtle shading to any character he played.

Looking at Burr's test reel for Hamilton Burger is a real eye-opener. Had he been chosen instead of William Talman, it's obvious that we would have had a very different DA. Burr easily dominates the audition as Burger, leaving the hapless character actor Tod Andrews, who plays Mason, in the dust.

William Hopper is a talented performer and his test for the Mason role shows him to excellent advantage.

Hopper's Perry Mason is quite personable, especially when trading lines with Ray Collins. His Perry Mason shows little surprise when he finds that Lt. Tragg has let himself into the law office and he easily keeps his cool as Tragg grills him about potential evidence tampering.

But the clearest contrast between Burr's interpretation of Perry Mason and William Hopper's comes in the courtroom scene. The audition script is exactly the same for both men. The actress playing the witness is the same too. She's Roxanne Arlen, frequently seen at the time as the "sexy bad girl" in TV dramas. (She later appeared in two episodes of the "Mason" show—"The Case of the Moth-Eaten Mink" and "The Case of the Jealous Journalist.")

On the audition reel, Arlen is a tough-cookie who's been carrying out a con with her common law husband. As Perry, Hopper conducts a low-key cross-examination of her, but doesn't miss a trick when it comes to tripping her up.

Hopper, as Perry, cross-examines Arlen

Oddly, when Hopper wants to hammer home a point in questioning Arlen, he almost seems to be trying too hard. It's as if he steps out of his nice guy character and feels uncomfortable with it.

But when Burr tackles the same courtroom scene, we understand why Gardner was so impressed. Hopper reads the lines with conviction, but Burr makes them come alive with his own expressive interpretation.

Slimmed-down Burr in same audition scene

Questioning Arlen, he pauses at the end of a sentence, his eyes moving slowly as if to carefully consider what he's just heard. When the witness makes a triumphant pronouncement, confident that she has stumped the attorney, Burr gives a friendly smile that turns into an amused smirk, just before he opens up with both-barrels, pounding on the witness stand rail and proving the woman a liar!

One of the bigger movies of 1951 was the Montgomery Clift/Elizabeth Taylor vehicle, "A Place in the Sun." This one has the actor playing a standout role on the right side of the law for a change, but even here some of his "bad guy" mannerisms come into play. In fact, as a district attorney hell bent on convicting Montgomery Clift of murder, Burr is downright scary in some scenes.

His emotional cross-examination of Clift is a dramatic highlight of the film. Burr has a rowboat that figures in the case brought into court.

Burr bullies Clift into taking part in a re-creation of the drowning death of Shelley Winters. It's virtually impossible to forget the scene where Burr demonstrates his version of the drowning. He brandishes an oar and slams it down with such force that it breaks in two.

Unsympathetic as he was though, his part in "A Place in the Sun" played a major role in his eventual selection as TV's "Perry Mason." Producer Gail Patrick Jackson had been impressed with the actor's performance as the DA and that's where she originally got the idea to test him for the part of Hamilton Burger.

Gail Patrick Jackson

Gail was a lovely woman who had a successful career as an actress, but she decided to get out of movies in the late forties and devote her time to business ventures. Her husband at the time was Cornwell Jackson, the literary agent for Erle Stanley Gardner.

Erle Stanley Gardner

As I mentioned earlier, Raymond Burr told me Gardner hated the old "Perry Mason" films and wanted to make sure that, if he ever sold rights to the character again, he would have control over how his famous lawyer was depicted.

Television was the hot new medium at this time and Gardner saw the potential for a tremendous new revenue stream. But he wasn't going to trust just anybody to set up a deal that would protect his interests. He already trusted Cornwell Jackson to handle his publishing empire and the fact that Jackson's wife had a long list of Hollywood connections provided the author with a perfect solution. Gardner got together with Gail and her husband to form a company that would produce the TV show.

THE CASE OF THE COLORFUL CO-STARS

As we know, while Raymond Burr initially tried out for the Burger role, it was Bill Talman who wound up with the part. And even though Bill Hopper auditioned to play Perry, the producers decided he'd be better as Paul Drake. Both casting decisions were major pluses for the show, because they meant Burr would be supported by two experienced and talented male actors.

Talman was known for his dynamic performances in some powerful film noirs, and Bill Hopper had the role of "easy-going second-lead" down pat from his various movie appearances. While it's true that Hopper took time out from acting to sell cars for a while, both of these guys were seasoned pros. And the same goes in spades for Barbara Hale.

Barbara had appeared in scores of movies and TV shows before being chosen to play Della Street. And, of course, Barbara was the co-star mentioned most often in the many stories published during the show's run, about Burr's friendship with other cast members.

I had read many of these articles, so I was well aware that the two were close, but I didn't realize *how* close until Burr brought up the subject when we were talking. It turned out the actor's relationship with Barbara and her husband, Bill Williams, went way back, almost to the beginning of Ray's movie career.

"I've known Barbara and Bill since they first met," said Burr. "We were all under contract to RKO.

Bill Williams and Barbara Hale at RKO

"Barbara is always a joy to work with," Burr said. "We worked together after the 'Perry Masons'—Barbara was on an

'Ironside' episode—and we see each other quite often."

The actor was quick to point out that Bill Williams appeared in several of Perry's cases. I told him I was aware of that and let him know that the one I found most fascinating was "The Case of the 12th Wildcat," in which Williams played a sleazy drunk. Burr laughed when I kidded him about how disillusioned I was seeing this episode as a kid, because Bill Williams had been one of my childhood heroes. He had starred in the early TV series "Kit Carson!"

Burr knew the real man behind "Kit Carson" as a good friend and occasional co-worker. He told me he might visit Bill, Barbara and the kids at their home on a day off, and then have the pleasure of working with the couple on a Mason episode the next week. "Back when we started the show, Barbara's children were very, very young. They've all grown-up now. I used to have little William Katt on my knee." (Bill Williams' real last name was Katt.)

By the time Raymond made the new Perry Mason two-hour TV movies, "Little William Katt" was old enough to be playing Paul Drake Junior in them! Again, it was a family affair, and the only regret Burr said he had was that Bill Williams wasn't able to work on the new shows. He told me Williams had a serious accident. If I remember correctly it occurred on a farm or ranch that he and Barbara Hale owned and involved unloading or stacking logs.

In any event, the discussion of Williams brought up the fate of other actors on "Perry Mason," including some of Burr's co-stars on the show. We talked about how he tried to get Bill Talman back on the program after the actor who played Hamilton Burger was fired by CBS. Burr rallied support for Talman and, along with producer Gail Patrick Jackson and others, lobbied CBS to allow him to return.

Talman was caught in a pot raid along with several other allegedly naked people, which led CBS to invoke its morals clause against the actor in March of 1960. Even though the charges were eventually thrown out, he wasn't allowed back on the show until December of that year.

It couldn't have been an easy time for the actor. Virtually blackballed, the long months of unemployment didn't stop the clock on the alimony and support payments that he owed to two ex-wives. Even when working on the show, while he had an excellent salary for the time, it wasn't close to what Burr was receiving. So it was a real blessing that Burr and his other co-stars made sure Bill Talman was re-hired, and his return was welcomed by fans.

Of course, much of Bill Talman's story was already known, including his battle with cancer and his brave appearance in an anti-smoking ad. Like most fans, I was quite aware of his post "Perry Mason" days and admired him greatly.

The co-star I hadn't heard much about was William Hopper. He was the actor who came immediately to mind when Raymond Burr talked with me about how well the "Perry Mason" cast got along. He always looked like the kind of guy it would be fun to hang around with.

At the time, there wasn't much information out there about his post-Perry Mason days. Come to think of it, there doesn't seem to be a heck of a lot more available now.

Of course I knew that the actor, one of my favorites, had been in films for years. As a kid I had seen him with Robert Mitchum in "Track of the Cat" at the local drive-in. The future Paul Drake even grew a beard for the role.

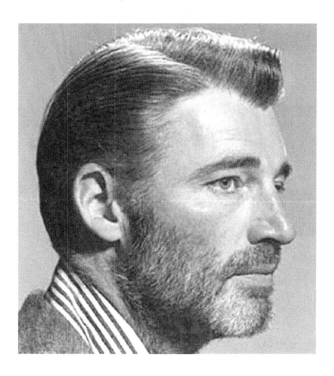

Hopper with beard for "Track of the Cat"

Director William Wellman, who helmed the 1954 film,

liked Hopper and featured him in several movies. On TV I'd seen him in "Mystery House," one of the better entries in the 1930's "Clue Club" series from Warner Brothers.

My other Hopper favorite was "20 Million Miles to Earth." I was an adolescent by the time that one came out and—like all my friends—I was thrilled by the Ray Harryhausen special effects in the movie. But, whether appearing in a sci-fi film or a more conventional drama, Hopper always looked debonair.

I knew the usual background stuff about Hopper's younger days. He was the son of actress Hedda Hopper, who later became a famous Hollywood columnist. She split with her husband when the boy was young and encouraged him to pursue an acting career. I had the impression that she was pushy and he was easy going.

Other than that, I was aware that Hopper stayed with the series for the entire run and had gone into semi-retirement after the program ended in 1966. (He only appeared in one movie after the series left the air, the dreadful "Myra Breckenridge," in which he looked older than his 54 years.)

There were reports that Hopper, who had a troubled relationship with his mother Hedda, tried to deal with stress by drinking. Whether that's true or not, Bill didn't appear to age well during the course of the show.

Hopper was looking older than his age

Hedda was the ultimate "stage mother." Married to matinee idol De Wolf Hopper, she had a lackluster career of her own, mostly in low-budget quickies, although I do remember seeing her in "Dracula's Daughter" when I was a kid. She divorced De Wolf when young bill was only a child and—when her film assignments eventually dwindled—she found work as a gossip columnist.

But Hedda's movie ambitions never really died. She just superimposed them on her son and tried to live her dreams through him. She sought publicity for Bill from an early age.

Hedda giving Bill exposure on her radio show

Despite attempts by Hedda to make Bill in her own image, he simply wasn't a pushy person. It would appear life in the limelight simply wasn't his thing and it took a toll.

William Hopper, the man who most of America knew and loved as Paul Drake on "Perry Mason," was only 55 when he died in 1970. I asked Raymond Burr what happened.

"It was sad ... very sad," he told me. I remember Burr talking about Hopper having some kind of breathing problem. I got the impression that he had seen Hopper when he was ill and that he felt smoking had something to do with his illness.

It was only after the internet came along that I was able to look up different accounts of Bill Hopper's death and they all seemed to agree that he suffered a stroke and died several weeks later of pneumonia. The only other person I could find who apparently agreed that smoking was, at least in part, responsible, was Gail Patrick Jackson. The actress-turned-"Perry Mason"- producer went way back with Hopper. They were both under contract to Paramount in the thirties, when Gail was a star and Bill was a bit player in films like "Murder with Pictures."

Gail Patrick as star, Bill Hopper as extra

Gail Patrick Jackson blamed smoking not just for Bill Hopper's early demise, but for the deaths of Ray Collins and Bill Talman as well.

Whatever problems William Hopper may have had in his personal life (and it couldn't have been easy growing up with someone like Hedda as your mom,) few would deny that he made the perfect Paul Drake. And I, for one, will always remember him knocking on the back door of Perry's office, quickly entering, perching on the desk, and greeting Della with a cheery "Hi beautiful!"

THE CASE OF THE ROSE-COLORED GLASSES

"It was like wiping out 20 years of not altogether good times."— Raymond Burr

The above quote is something Raymond Burr said when the two of us were discussing his first "Perry Mason" two-hour TV movie. The full quote referred to the initial day of shooting the new show with Barbara Hale.

"What's interesting," he told me, "is that we started filming the first new show on a courtroom set, and it was like wiping out 20 years of not altogether good times, just 20 years of your life so that you were immediately 20 years younger."

When actors make the rounds to promote a new film or TV show, they get used to pretty much saying the same thing over and over again, so I'm sure the "Wiping out 20 years" wasn't unique to our conversation. But the "20 years of *not altogether good times*," was another matter. Perhaps it's because, before we began the formal interview, we talked a bit about the nostalgic appeal of the original show.

Lots of things, both good and bad, had taken place between the time the original "Perry Mason" show ended and the announcement of the new "Perry Mason Mystery Movies." Raymond had another hit series with "Ironside" and many other show business triumphs, but some of his other projects weren't as successful. He had the comfort of knowing he had brought joy to so many servicemen during the Korean and Vietnam Wars, but he also saw the pain many of these men suffered.

There were big, headline-making changes during this period and there were smaller, gradual changes that affected the fabric of American life. All of us went through personal changes too. Maybe that's why watching the program today feels so comfortable. It provides an instant trip back in time.

So I specifically asked Raymond whether times really were different back in the days when he was starring in "Perry Mason." Here was that rare opportunity to get the answer from the "Horse's Mouth," so to speak. Even before I asked, though, I pretty much knew what the answer would be. As I go back over my notes, I can see it in the way I couched the question:

"When I watch the 'Perry Mason' shows, for me they're filled with nostalgia because it seems like a more simple time. Something tells me that you're going to burst my bubble and tell me that was not the case, but I'll ask anyway. Were times then just as difficult as they are now?" The actor paused to give the question some thought, and then answered.

"I think they probably were. I think we had the explosion of all the rapid changes in the late sixties, but we were getting into vast change in the fifties too. You have to think of rock music coming in during the fifties and into the sixties, of course. In the late sixties and seventies the changes were rapid, but (in the fifties) it just wasn't as evident. There was just less publicity about it. Television wasn't as prevalent then."

I believe there's a great deal of wisdom in that answer and, looking back, I'm amazed that the actor only took 30 seconds or so to consider the question and come up with his response.

It's absolutely true that changes taking place in the fifties got much less publicity. We're bombarded with 24-hour cable news and digital reports on the internet these days, neither of which even existed back then.

And Burr was one of the first people I ever met who cited the rise of rock in the fifties as being a precursor of later changes in the sixties and seventies. He was, as usual, quite right. If you didn't live through it, the extent of the upheaval is hard to imagine. That's because viewing the "rock revolution" from the present day doesn't make the huge shift in attitudes it engendered clear.

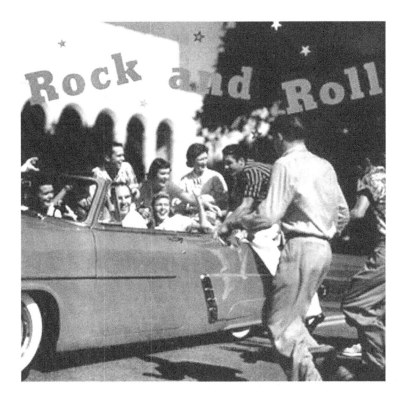

Raymond Burr was in his thirties when the music began to change. That's why, I'm sure, it was top of mind when I asked him about what many of us think of as the relatively staid fifties. Burr had grown up in the big band era and the music of the early fifties wasn't all that different. By 1954, Rosemary Clooney, Eddie Fisher and Patti Page were sharing the charts with Bill Haley and His Comets. But by 1956, Elvis Presley had hit the music scene with full force. "Heartbreak Hotel," "Hound Dog," and "Don't Be Cruel" were at the top of the charts. Meanwhile, other early rockers like Carl Perkins, Fats Domino and Gene Vincent were making inroads as well. By the end of the fifties easy listening performers were virtually banished from the top ten.

Baby boomers like myself barely remember this, but a perceptive man like Burr was probably old enough and wise enough to see this radical transformation for what it was: Nothing short of a massive generational shift to a culture of youth. For better or worse, it shaped the future of American life and—as Burr pointed out—it was at least as important as some of the events of the late sixties that get so much more publicity.

Also, after talking with Burr, I came to understand that my rose-colored view of the days when he was filming the show couldn't possibly be totally realistic. For starters, so many of the things I knew to be true about the people on the show should have convinced me that times couldn't have been all that simple back in the fifties and sixties. Raymond Burr must have had concerns about the circumstances of his private life being revealed. While mainstream publications were far less salacious than many of today's newspapers, there were always the bottom-feeders like "Confidential," "Exposed," "The Low Down," and others.

And Burr's co-stars on the show certainly weren't without problems. In addition to Bill Talman's pot bust, heavy drinking reportedly led to the breakup of a couple marriages and heavy smoking led to the cancer that claimed his life. Burr thought Talman was one of the best actors in the business and many would agree with him. I suspect Raymond had a special appreciation of Talman because both of their pre-"Perry Mason" careers involved similar types of roles in similar kinds of films.

While Talman hadn't achieved the same level of success

that helped Burr win roles in so many movies, the 15 or so films the future Hamilton Burger made before getting hired for "Perry Mason," showed he had the acting chops necessary to take on any role.

Like Burr, though, casting directors seemed to favor Talman as a heavy. Also like Burr, his movie credits were weighted toward film noir. And he was at his best playing bad guys in classics like "The Hitch-Hiker" and "City That Never Sleeps."

Early publicity portrait of Bill Talman

Prior to "Perry Mason," Talman was beginning to get a

decent amount of TV work, and landing the Burger role provided a regular salary. But he had a family to support, and the season he was banished from "Mason" put a big dent in his finances.

Talman never had a conventional face for films, even in his youth. But he did have an expressiveness that was perfect for character parts. Like Burr, had it not been for "Perry Mason," he might have wound up playing bad guys for the rest of his career.

The talented Ray Collins, who played the intrepid Lt. Tragg, had to cope with health issues as well.

Collins, a show business veteran who had been part of Orson Welles' Mercury Theater, was considerably older than the rest of the regulars when the series began in 1957. In addition to his health problems, he would soon have trouble remembering lines. At a 2014 symposium, Barbara Hale mentioned that Collins had asked her to run his lines with him prior to shooting scenes—something she said she was more than happy to do. But the actor's age was taking a toll.

By 1961 Collins' emphysema was growing worse and a new character, Lt. Andy Anderson (played by Wesley Lau,) was brought in to lighten his load. Collins made his final "Perry Mason" appearance on a show that aired in early 1964. He died of emphysema in 1965.

As I looked at the problems faced by the program's main cast members, I began to realize that "Perry Mason" didn't really exist in some perfect past just beyond the reach of today's viewers. Times may have been better, but they were far from ideal. And the stars of the show definitely weren't the only ones who had to deal with difficult circumstances.

The personal lives of many others who appeared on the series were often fraught with challenges too. The beautiful Joanna Moore, who was featured in 1958's "The Case of the Terrified Typist" and 1963's "The Case of the Reluctant Model," was married to Ryan O'Neal, who was also featured on the show (1964's "The Case of the Bountiful Beauty.") But Joanna lost custody of her children, Tatum and Griffin, reportedly due to addiction problems. The children later had much-publicized troubles of their own.

Alcohol, then as now, claimed lives. The beautiful Peggy Castle, who co-starred in 1957's "The Case of the Negligent Nymph," was among the guest stars who reportedly died of cirrhosis. She was only forty-five years old.

Judy Tyler, the striking young "Howdy Doody" actress who appeared in 1957's "The Case of the Fan Dancer's Horse," died in a car accident before the program even aired. The 24 year old actress, who began her career as a teenage dancer at the Copacabana, was also awaiting the release of her Elvis Presley film "Jailhouse Rock."

Karyn Kupcinet, a young actress who was the daughter of columnist Irv Kupcinet, was killed in her West Hollywood apartment in 1963. Her last on-screen appearance was in "The Case of the Capering Camera," which didn't air until after her unsolved murder.

And, going back over the long list of guest stars on "Perry Mason," I was amazed to realize how many had actually taken their own lives. Veteran actor Grant Withers, once briefly married to Loretta Young, appeared in "The Case of the Gilded Lilly," which aired in the spring of 1958.

Grant Withers with William Hopper

In March of 1959 Withers committed suicide—a sad end to a career that began as a leading man in silent pictures. He was only 54 and suffering from health problems.

And Everett Sloane, the extremely talented actor who appeared in 1962's "The Case of the Poison Pen-Pal," was only 55 and concerned about losing his eyesight, when he died of a barbiturate overdose. Don "Red" Barry, who appeared with Raymond on "Perry Mason" (1964's "The Case of the Simple Simon") and was later featured on several episodes of "Ironside," took his own life in 1980. Barry, who got his nickname from the "Red Ryder" serial he made for Republic in the forties, committed suicide after a domestic dispute.

Gary Vinson, who appeared in "The Case of the Drowning Duck," shot and killed himself in Redondo Beach, California in 1984. He was only 47. Carolyn Craig, a co-star in the "Drowning Duck" episode was only 36 when she reportedly died of a gunshot wound. Richard Webb, who was in both 1963's "The Case of the Velvet Claws" and 1965's "The Case of the Impetuous Imp," took his own life, as did Stanley Adams, who appeared in 1964's "The Case of the Missing Button."

Sam Buffington who was featured in 1959's "The Case of the Foot-Loose Doll," was only 28 years old when he committed suicide. Kate Manx who co-starred in 1963's "The Case of the Nebulous Nephew," was only 34 when she took an overdose in 1964.

Members of the acting profession seem more prone to suicide than the general population, but I was still surprised to find the long list of "Mason" performers in that category. It was a vivid reminder that, at least for some, times were difficult back then too.

And the TV show really did mimic the times ... the good and the bad. It seems strange to see so much smoking going on. And several episodes make it clear that the cocktail hour was every bit as common back then, as the family ritual of soccer moms loading the kids into their SUVs is today.

So, I'm afraid I've had to give up some of my illusions about *everything* being so much better in the "good old days." But I still feel that way about *some* things when I watch the show. I think there was a very real pride in America that's sadly lacking these days—a belief that things would be much improved for the next generation and we could accomplish our goals. There was a sense that things were getting better instead of worse.

I think that "can do" attitude is best exemplified by—of all things—the cars! I don't know anyone who doesn't experience at least a twinge of wistfulness when viewing the fantastic old autos on the show. How can you not love an era that promoted the theory of "Bigger is Better" with unbridled optimism in car ads like the one below for Ford.

IN 2 NEW SUPER SIZES

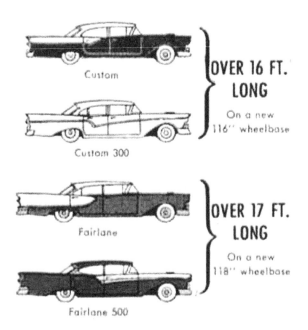

Custom

OVER 16 FT. LONG

On a new 116'' wheelbase

Custom 300

Fairlane

OVER 17 FT. LONG

On a new 118'' wheelbase

Fairlane 500

The cars driven by the main characters on "Perry Mason," not surprisingly, depended on whether Ford or General Motors was sponsoring the show.

Burr, at various times, drove a 1957 Ford Fairlane 500 Skyliner and a '57 Cadillac de Ville convertible. Later, he was tooling around in a Lincoln Continental convertible.

Bill Hopper, with Burr at the wheel, in '57 Cadillac

Early on, William Hopper as Paul Drake was behind the wheel of a 1957 Ford Thunderbird, and later he drove a '57 Corvette convertible, but T-birds appeared to be his ride of choice for most of the series. What a difference compared to the cookie-cutter cars that clutter today's highways.

And it's not just the main characters zipping around in classy cars. It always fun to spot a supporting player in a cool set of wheels. How about a 1961 Buick Electra convertible? Perhaps you prefer a curiosity like the Edsel (ah—Ford had such high hopes for that one!) Yes, looking back to the days when those now-collectable cars were common (and gas was cheap) definitely fuels part of the nostalgic attraction of the program for me.

But it isn't just the distinctive car designs or the mid-century modern furnishings that catch our attention. The lifestyles of the characters in the fifties and sixties play a significant role in the show's popularity too, and so do the people who portray those characters. It's always fun to spot up-and-coming actors before they became stars, like a pre-"I Dream of Jeannie" Barbara Eden.

A very young Barbara Eden

Barbara appeared way back in the show's first season. She played the daughter of a woman accused of murder in 1957's "The Case of the Angry Mourner."

And Robert Redford visited the show on his way to future movie mega-stardom. He appeared in 1960's "The Case of the Treacherous Toupee."

Redford had the "star look" even back then

Redford and Eden were just a few of the performers who went on to bigger things. The beautiful Angie Dickinson, who would later star in the TV series "Police Woman" and popular films such as "Dressed to Kill," co-starred in the

1958 entry "The Case of the One-Eyed Witness."

In 1959, George TaKei—who would go on to play Sulu on "Star Trek"—made one of his first TV appearances in "The Case of the Blushing Pearls." In fact, "Perry Mason" was a virtual bullpen for "Star Trek" actors-in-training. DeForest Kelley, who played "Bones" McCoy on the show, was in "The Case of the Unwelcome Bride" and future Dr. Spock Leonard Nimoy had a run-in with Raymond in "The Case of the Shoplifter's Shoe."

There were so many others who also gained valuable experience on "Perry Mason," ranging from a very young Burt Reynolds to "Man from Uncle" co-star David McCallum. And even supporting players whose names we may not know tend to become like old friends as we see them over and over again in various roles. It's all part and parcel of the show's lasting charm.

THE CASE OF THE BEWILDERING BIOGRAPHIES

Back when the original TV program was a big hit on CBS, like many fans, I got my "Perry Mason" fix between weekly shows by reading TV magazines and newspaper articles about the series. But they only sparked my determination to find out more about the man who brought Perry Mason to life.

That's because so many of the articles about Raymond Burr were confusing and contradictory. The stories fell into a couple of main categories.

There was lots of coverage of Burr and his co-stars. Sometimes writers would focus on Bill Talman and ask how he felt about his character constantly losing. Of course, publicity was guaranteed when he finally appeared to win.

At other times there would be stories about Barbara Hale's early years at RKO, her marriage to fellow-actor Bill Williams, and how much she enjoyed working with Raymond. There was also the usual "Puff Stuff"—several magazines, for example, ran pieces on what a practical joker the actor was on the set. The stories were true, but they were the typical cutesy things that public relations people latch on to and then feed to the press to try to get as much "ink" as possible.

But then there were the stories that really intrigued me ... the ones about the star's personal life. They were real tear-jerkers and when I read them at the time, I remember feeling so sorry for this successful actor who had gotten so many bad breaks. If these articles were to be believed, Raymond Burr had been married three times and two of his wives had passed away—one in a plane crash, the other from cancer. As if that wasn't enough, we were told the actor's young son had died of leukemia. But there was always something hard to believe about this sad scenario. The stories didn't quite ring true, especially as I got older.

In the late sixties, "Inside TV" magazine ran an unusual article questioning many of the inaccurate press releases about Raymond Burr. It was an excellent investigative piece and the author took the time to speak with people who knew Burr and carefully check dates. The article came to the conclusion that much of the material had been made up. This writer was way ahead of his time and bucking the trend, since most TV magazines were simply repeating the same old stories.

But the author also said that Burr detested interviews about his personal life, steered clear of the working press, and almost never granted interviews. If that was the case, he certainly mellowed in later years. Then again, it may have depended on who he was speaking with and how comfortable he felt.

I remembered the actor being quite candid about his private life. I even recalled the two of us discussing a common medication we both took, which would hardly be the kind of topic someone wary of mentioning personal issues would bring up. So my overall impression, even though it had been decades since I had talked with him, was that he had spoken more like a friendly, everyday guy than a "star." In checking my files for this book, I was pleasantly surprised to find my memory hadn't deceived me.

For example, something got us talking about long plane flights and that led into a discussion of his island retreat in Fiji. He mentioned that he loved the place, but getting there and back was beginning to take a toll.

And then he said something that, looking back on it now, makes me feel he was growing less secretive about his private life, at least when in an informal setting. He told me he was purchasing a new property with his friend.

"We had the orchid garden on the island," he said. "That's what everybody talks about." "But," he added, "we've bought a couple of farms next to each other up in northern California. It's a little easier than going back and forth to the island."

The friend, of course, was Raymond Burr's longtime companion Robert Benevides. The farms eventually became the Raymond Burr Vineyards, which the two men cultivated.

I saw a television interview with the actor a couple of years after we had spoken, in which he was asked about both the Fiji island retreat and the northern California property and at no time did he make any mention of a friend being involved. So I do think he was very careful how he spoke and with whom he spoke.

I had known nothing about Burr's sexual orientation, nor did I care. And, if I did know, I certainly wouldn't have made it public. Over the years I was privy to several so-called "secrets" involving stars, mostly because I just happened to be with them when something came up—perhaps an urgent call concerning a son or daughter's drug use or something similar. My attitude on that sort of thing was always the same: It was nobody's business.

After he passed away, the details of Raymond Burr's private life did come out, as people tried to make sense of the various tall tales that had been told over the years. Initially, some tribute articles still included those stories of family tragedy that had surfaced so often.

Raymond Burr never mentioned anything at all to me about having three ex-wives or a son. As far as I know, he was married only once, in 1947 to actress Isabella Ward. They separated early on and finally divorced in 1952.

Those publicity stories about multiple wives and a son who died may have been dreamed-up at some point to try to guard Raymond's private life. Looking back, it's amazing that these tales were accepted for so many years, but the publicity mill kept repeating them during the original run of the series. I always thought Burr actually wanted to jettison them early on, but it appears he and his staff continued to occasionally mention them throughout the years, right up until his death.

So was there a deeper reason Raymond Burr kept telling such tall tales? I think perhaps there was. The Academy Award-winning actor George Kennedy was a friend of Burr's. Kennedy was another one of my favorite interviews. They were both big guys—Burr was around six feet tall, Kennedy was about three inches taller. But I never felt intimidated because they were both so easy to talk with. And the two of them had acted together on both the "Perry

Mason" and "Ironside" shows.

Raymond Burr and George Kennedy on "Ironside"

I believe Raymond and George had something else in common as well. Both were lonely when they were children.

Kennedy was raised by his mother, but she had to work most of the time to support her child and herself. To deal with the loneliness he'd listen to the radio, act out the parts played on various radio shows and keep himself company as best he could. Burr had to deal with the divorce of his mother and father at an early age and a mother who seems to have left a good deal of Raymond's parenting to his grandparents. He apparently kept to himself at school because he was teased about his weight. This was a perfect breeding ground for fantasy and it may have been at this juncture that Raymond began to develop the tendency to embellish that led to some of his more outlandish publicity tales.

Much like reports of a romance with Natalie Wood in the fifties, these stories kept surfacing. At least the Wood rumor had some basis in fact. She and Burr became close when the two appeared in "A Cry in the Night" in 1956.

Burr and Wood in "A Cry in the Night"

More than 20 years younger than Burr, it would appear Natalie was impressed by the knowledge and sophistication of this sensitive older man. She may well have hoped that a romantic relationship would develop, but that was hardly likely to happen. In any event, Warner Brothers had other plans. They wanted Natalie to be seen dating Tab Hunter. A younger couple would get more coverage in the Teen magazines and Hunter needed all the help he could get in portraying a more masculine image.

Had Natalie seen the Hollywood premier of the film "A Star Is Born," just a year prior to the start of filming on "A Cry in the Night," she might have realized how slim her chances were with Raymond Burr. Virtually all of the major celebrities of the day were on hand for the event. In addition to Judy Garland, the star of the movie, those in attendance included Elizabeth Taylor, Debbie Reynolds, Dean Martin, Joan Crawford, Kim Novak, Dorothy Lamour, Alan Ladd, Lucille Ball and Desi Arnaz, Lauren Bacall, Doris Day, Mamie Van Doren, Tony Curtis and Janet Leigh—in short, just about everyone who was anyone in Hollywood.

Keeping this dazzling display of motion picture royalty in mind, watching contemporary coverage of the premier is telling. Shortly after William Hopper's gossip-columnist mother Hedda is introduced, Raymond is brought up to the microphone with a sailor named Frank Vitti in tow. He introduces the sailor as having just come back from Korea but even so, it's bizarre to see this young man showing up at a gala reserved for Hollywood stars. In the early "Perry Mason" years, the young man was identified as Burr's "assistant" in some articles and as his "nephew" in others.

I came across a piece on Raymond in a 1959 edition of "The Australian Women's Weekly." ("Perry Mason" was big "down under," and—as I mention elsewhere—Burr spoke with me about singing on a tour of Australia.)

One of the pictures accompanying the article shows Burr in front of a fireplace with a man and a young woman. The same picture appeared in the U.S. where the principals were properly identified. But in the Australian paper the photo is captioned, "With his teenage niece and nephew Phyllis and Frank Vitti." Phyllis was his real niece but of course her last name *wasn't* Vitti. Frank's name *was* real, but he didn't look much like a teenage "nephew" in his white short-sleeve shirt exposing hairy arms, his white chinos, and white moccasins with no socks.

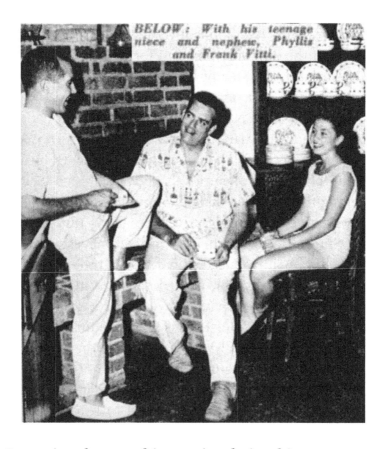

I mention the way this 1950's relationship was portrayed only because I think it helps explain the more extreme publicity stories about Burr's background. Despite what the actor told me about vast changes in the fifties, those changes didn't extend to the acceptance of alternative lifestyles.

THE CASE OF THE B-MOVIE BARRISTER

Before he became the world's most famous lawyer, Raymond Burr appeared in some classic clunkers! Ask any actor who's done a substantial number of films and they'll tell you that meaty roles in major films come up only so often. Every movie can't be a "Rear Window" or "A Place in the Sun." And that basic law of Hollywood reality held for Raymond too. The difference with Burr is that he had a sense of humor about it.

It's a good thing he did because, again, my misspent youth watching old movies came into play as I was talking with the actor. I couldn't keep myself from teasing him about a couple of less-than-memorable films.

"You know," I said, "I've seen you in so many really good movies, that I hope you won't mind me bringing up a couple of fairly bad ones. I'm thinking of 'Love Happy' with The Marx Brothers and 'Bride of the Gorilla' with Lon Chaney Junior!" Far from being unhappy, Burr just laughed and said, "No, No, No ... all those pictures I did are showing today on television!" He shook his head and smiled, as if to say "What can you do ... they play the bad along with the good!"

"Love Happy" was the last and worst of The Marx Brothers films, notable only for a walk-on appearance by a young Marilyn Monroe. Burr actually gives a very good performance considering the fact that he has to deal with lines like, "She's giving him the whammy," as lovely Ilona Massey tries to put Harpo under her spell.

And 1951's "Bride of the Gorilla" was a horror quickie of the "Potted-Palm-Jungle" variety. Burr plays a plantation owner who falls under a native curse.

"Bride" couldn't have been a very happy set. Shot on the cheap in only a little over a week, the film's leading lady, Barbara Peyton, was on a downward alcoholic spiral that would eventually lead to her being charged with soliciting for prostitution.

Peyton with Burr in "Bride of the Gorilla"

Meanwhile, co-stars Lon Chaney Junior and Tom Conway were struggling with drinking problems as well. Two years after "Bride," Conway and Burr would appear together again in "Tarzan and the She Devil." And Barbara Hale had worked with Conway on two "Falcon" pictures when they were both at RKO and he was a leading man.

Hale, Burr and others on "Perry Mason" were glad the program could give Conway a hand many years later by hiring him for a 1964 episode of the show. But his alcoholism continued to progress and, by 1967, Conway was dead. The story is a sad one and I bring it up only because Conway was just one of many actors who had fallen on hard times that found work on the "Perry Mason" series.

Burr also reportedly tried to help Barbara Peyton get a role on the show. However her brushes with the law were making headlines and the producers apparently didn't want to risk it.

One of the many people Burr and producer Gail Patrick Jackson *did* find plenty of work for was George E. Stone, the veteran actor who appeared with Chester Morris in the "Boston Blackie" movies. After he became ill, they hired Stone for the non-stressful part of court clerk on the Mason series. The recurring role assured the character actor of a source of income.

And there were so many other old-timers that showed up on "Perry Mason." They included familiar faces like silent great Francis X. Bushman, thirties leading man Regis Toomey, cowboy star Johnny Mack Brown, Brian Donlevy, Edgar Buchanan, serial star Bruce Bennett, Dick Foran, Jon Hall of Universal's Maria Montez epics and "Ramar of the Jungle," John Archer, who co-starred in the cult classic "King of the Zombies," Lynn Bari, Zasu Pitts, Stuart Erwin, Ann Rutherford, Jeff Donnell, Former "Dead End Kid" Billy Halop, Reed Hadley of "Zorro's Fighting Legion" fame, Douglas Fowley, Lyle Talbot, Minerva Urecal, former child star Jackie Coogan, Lloyd Corrigan, Jerome Cowan, Frankie Darro, Robert Armstrong and Fay Wray of "King Kong" fame, and scores of other "old pros."

Burr had worked with Fay Wray in the movie "Crime of Passion," appeared with Regis Toomey in "Great Day in the Morning," Minerva Urecal in "A Man Alone," Jeff Donnell in

"The Blue Gardenia," and Douglas Fowley in "Horizons West" and "Desperate."

Douglas Fowley and Burr in "Desperate"

The long list of movie veterans who found work on "Perry Mason" makes one thing very obvious. If Raymond Burr knew you from his pre-"Perry Mason" days, he wasn't going to forget you now that he was a star!

THE CASE OF THE GANGBUSTERS VS GODZILLA

The pre-"Perry Mason" days included Ray's insert shots for the American version of "Godzilla." The film was a big money-maker when it was released and is considered a cult classic today. But nobody knew it would be a hit when Burr was shooting his scenes for the movie. And few would have predicted that a film featuring a guy in a rubber suit as its main attraction, would have become such a box office draw!

In "Godzilla" Burr plays an American wire service reporter in Tokyo. His main job is to provide a running English-language narration of Godzilla's rampage, by dictating into his tape recorder while Tokyo supposedly burns.

Remember, it hadn't been all that long since Burr had put

in such a powerful performance in "Rear Window." And here he was going into something shot strictly on the cheap. Although they later sold it to Joseph E. Levine for distribution, the two guys who bought the movie from its Japanese owners were Richard Kay and Harry Rybnick, who specialized in cheesy exploitation pictures like "Untamed Women," "Live Fast, Die Young," and "Girls on the Loose." Since they were producing the US inserts, you knew this wasn't going to be a big bucks shoot!

Burr didn't suffer any ill effects from appearing in this hastily-revamped monster movie aimed at kids. In fact he would soon land his career-defining role on "Perry Mason." The fact is Raymond Burr's participation in non-prestige projects simply didn't seem to matter in Hollywood.

Other actors weren't so lucky. "Bride of the Gorilla," which was made by independent producer Jack Broder comes to mind again. Broder also made the Grade Z, "Bela Lugosi Meets a Brooklyn Gorilla," and—yes—it's as bad as the title suggests. Poor Lugosi was on his way to such sad sagas as "Plan Nine from Outer Space," and all because he had a reputation as a "B" movie actor from all of his appearances in poverty row productions. From the beginning, when he was starring in "Dracula," he would keep alternating between major films at Universal and shoe-string productions like "White Zombie" for the Halperin Brothers.

But unlike Lugosi and many other actors, who were branded as "B" movie material after appearing in one too many low budget films, Ray seemed to have no trouble moving between "A" and "B" pictures. And, even though he joked with me about movies like "Bride of the Gorilla," he actually seemed to like "Godzilla."

At one point when I was talking with Burr about the original "Godzilla," he surprised me by saying he would be in a new Godzilla movie, essentially playing the same role. The film was eventually released under the title "Godzilla 1985." The new footage was shot at Raleigh Studios and they got all of the Burr material they needed in one day!

Raymond Burr in "Godzilla 1985"

Speaking of shooting all of Raymond's scenes in one day, just a brief aside to those who seem determined to challenge everything that the actor ever said to reporters. Some claim stories about Burr shooting all of his scenes for the original "Godzilla" in a 24 hour period are fabrications. They cite the director's son, who said it was more like three to five days.

The first thing that comes to mind is who cares? I don't know how long it took to shoot the American scenes, but I do know a one-day time frame is possible. It takes careful preparation, but Terry Morse—Supervising Film Editor and Director of the American footage—had plenty of experience. In fact, he was the editor on the 1935 Perry Mason film, "The Case of the Curious Bride." His Director of Photography, Guy Roe, had lots of experience too. He was responsible for the excellent camera work on, among other films, "Armored Car Robbery, with future Hamilton Burger William Talman.

And other details Raymond Burr gave about the filming of the American inserts were certainly quite accurate. He emphasized how small the studio was where they shot the scenes, and he wasn't kidding. Visual Drama Inc., as the studio was called, had only one other claim to fame. It was used to shoot indoor scenes on the early TV show, "Gang Busters." If you've ever seen the show, you'll notice just how cramped the sets look.

It doesn't appear that Visual Drama got a heck of a lot of

other work, but "Gangbusters" Producer William Faris and Production Manager Mack Wright would rent it out when they weren't shooting the show. The Director of Photography for "Gangbusters," Guy Roe, became the man behind the camera for the "Godzilla" scenes. And "Gangbusters" Film Editor, Terry Morse, became Director

The connection explains how one of Hollywood's smallest studios wound up being used for a movie about Japan's biggest monster. Inexpensive props and the power of suggestion were used in place of an actual location budget.

For example, Burr stands in the corner of the cramped studio, a calendar on the wall, a globe by his side and a Japanese brochure in his hand. And Bingo – he's an ace wire-service reporter in Tokyo! With this kind of cost-cutting, Burr could well be right about a one-day shoot.

Burr was also right about his professional choices, even though—from the outside—it may have looked as if he was courting career suicide by appearing in all of those "B" films and taking a chance on "Godzilla." As I mentioned earlier, he was one of the few actors who could move successfully between low-budget programmers at small studios and big-budget productions at major studios, because he was never really branded as a "B" actor.

In Britain, many of the folks in the business refer to themselves as "Jobbing Actors." It's a phrase that would apply to Raymond Burr too. As one British actor explained, "Look, I'm a working actor. It's what I do. I want to act. So, if a job presents itself, I'll probably take it. Does that mean I show up in some inferior films? Sure. But it also means I get a chance to appear in some excellent ones too."

It was the same with Raymond Burr. There's no way he could appear in the number of films he did between the mid-forties and the mid-fifties without some of them being clunkers. However, despite the fact that Burr made some less-than-stellar movies, I don't think casting directors at major studios cared. He was so good that he would stand head-and-shoulders above fellow-actors in auditions. And that was really all that ever mattered.

THE CASE OF THE LOQUACIOUS LOCATIONS

"Perry Mason" falls into a special category of TV show. Part of its charm lies in getting a rare glimpse into parts of our past. That's why so many fans keep an eye out for even brief scenes from the old shows that were shot outside the studio. The location shots "speak" to today's viewers about what those days were like.

And the reason there were often times when it was necessary to venture outside the studio was related to the size of the lots they were using for the show. Burr told me the production company shot at several facilities over the years and then, in rapid succession, he rattled off the different places they used as home base.

"We really moved around quite a bit," Burr said. "We were at Fox Western, Fox, General Service Studios, and then the last several years of "Perry Mason," we were at the old Chaplin Studios."

"Fox Western" wasn't, as it may sound, a lot where 20th Century Fox shot westerns. Instead, Burr was using the nickname for the very first Hollywood home of Fox Studios back in the silent days. It was located at the corner of Sunset Boulevard and *Western* Avenue, hence the name.

It was a small studio that Fox eventually used for its series pictures, like "Charlie Chan," "Mike Shayne" and "Mr. Moto." So it had a proud history of mystery movies behind it when "Mason" moved in. That was 1956, the first year that Fox, then filming features at its larger studio, began doing TV programs at the Western Avenue facility.

"Perry Mason" shot its first two seasons at the studio, which had almost nothing in the way of a backlot. The show did have access to the main Fox lot, but unless some special structure was called for, it was just as easy to shoot on the streets near Fox Western. That meant we got at least some location work in a few shows.

So we get to see Wilshire Blvd. (only 20 minutes from the studio) as it was back in the day and Grand Avenue (only 15 minutes away.) Shooting on Las Palmas and various tree-lined streets in Hancock Park was convenient as well, which means we get a nice slice of fifties and sixties homes via the show. Of course the rosy view of life portrayed by the mansion-like houses in Hancock Park is a bit misleading, since most of us couldn't have afforded those pricey houses back then and we can't afford them now!

Hancock Park home

And don't be fooled by the giant, white colonial mansion that puts even the Hancock Park homes to shame. This impressive building appears in several episodes, including "The Case of the Sulky Girl" and "The Case of the Black-Eyed

Blonde." But don't look for it on any Los Angeles map.

When Raymond Burr told me they had access to the larger facilities of 20ᵗʰ Century Fox proper, including the big backlot and the Fox ranch, I realized this was where the "Mason" team would go if they needed something special, and the outdoor mansion façade certainly filled the bill.

By end of the fifties, "Perry Mason" was based at General Service Studios, a relatively small rental facility, once again with no backlot to speak of. But General Service was perfect for independent production and had provided a home for many early television luminaries such as Lucille Ball and Desi Arnaz, George Burns and Gracie Allen, etc.

While Perry Mason was filming at General Service, from 1959 until 1962, studio buildings sometimes doubled for other locations and, if a movie studio is featured in the plot of an episode, take a close look because you're probably seeing the real front gate of General Service or nearby Desilu Cahuenga. In 1959's "The Case of the Artful Dodger" General Service "plays the part" of "Globe Film Corporation." So, when we see Burr at the guard gate of "Globe Studios," he's actually on the same lot he worked at every day for three years.

Perry at the fictitious "Globe Film Corporation"

And since, as I was quick to find out, Burr had a great sense of humor, he must have gotten a kick out of other "guest appearances" the studio made on the show. The real address of General Service—1040 North Las Palmas Avenue—is sometimes used as the address of fictional characters on the show in episodes like "The Case of the

Crying Cherub" and "The Case of the Lavender Lipstick" (both from 1960.)

Hopper, Talman & Burr at General Service Studios

Even when the program later moved to Chaplin Studios which, as Burr told me, was for the final three seasons, there still wasn't any real backlot to make life easier.

The Chaplin studio was steeped in history, and actors who worked there—including Jack Larson who played Jimmy Olsen on "Superman"—spoke with reverence about the atmosphere of the place. But the outdoor sets were long ago replaced by a parking lot. Shortly after the "Mason" team moved out, Herb Alpert bought the facility for use as a recording studio. Later, Jim Henson's company purchased the property.

Jim Henson's "Kermit the Frog" atop studio gates

In some ways, the fact that none of the studios that were used to shoot the show had backlots has been a blessing for today's "Perry Mason" fans. It forced the producers to go on location more frequently, and many of those outings provide a tantalizing glimpse of everyday mid-century living.

As I mentioned, the show sometimes shot a few scenes close to the studio or the producers would go just a little further afield and treat us to better known locations in LA.

One episode might show the old Mayflower Hotel on South Grand Avenue, while another might include a shot of

Park La Brea Towers. Plummer Park on Santa Monica Boulevard shows up in a couple of episodes too and we view the old headquarters of the Superior Oil Company doubling as the exterior of "The Brent Building," where Perry supposedly had his office.

We also see official sites like the Los Angeles County Courthouse and the Hall of Justice, most of which look basically the same now as they did then.

Meanwhile, if there's a beach scene in a "Perry Mason" episode you can count on seeing Leo Carrillo State Park and Paradise Cove. Of course saltwater wasn't the only soggy setting the producers sometimes needed, which is why Malibu Lake appears in several episodes of "Perry Mason." Most of the time, when the action takes place at a lake or even if there's just the need for an establishing shot of a lake, Malibu is first choice, since it was close. However, that wasn't always the case. Burr and company actually bit the bullet and journeyed to Big Bear Lake to the hamlet of Fawnskin—65 miles outside Los Angeles.

Actress Ina Victor with Burr in Fawnskin

The "Perry Mason" writers even used the town's real name in the Fawnskin episode, which was entitled "The Case of the Violent Village." As we shall soon see, it wasn't the only long-distance location shoot.

Given the sometimes short lead time between the shooting and airing of episodes and the difficulty of dealing with unanticipated events (For example, the broadcast of Bill Talman shows already in the can were delayed due to his pot bust) it really is a lucky break that we have as many location shoots as we do to enjoy in re-runs today.

And one of those locations—Redlands, California—stands out above all the others for me. That's because what it was like then—and events that have taken place *since* then—may provide the clearest explanation yet of why so many of us would like to return to "The World According to Perry Mason."

Yes, I know Raymond Burr told me every era comes with its own set of problems, and I'm sure he was right about that. But I wonder what he would have thought about some of the things we face today.

I'd like to draw a parallel between the real life changes that took place over the years at the location and the memories etched forever in our minds thanks to re-runs of the show shot there. It's called "The Case of the Brazen Bequest"—a 1961 episode with a college background.

As we shall see, Redlands, California may have been frozen in time on "Perry Mason," but it certainly wasn't immune to change in real life. Unfortunately, one of those changes involved a particular horror that Perry Mason never had to face: The stark reality of modern-day terrorism!

Raymond, Bill Hopper, Barbara Hale and other members of the cast and crew journeyed to Redlands in the fall of 1961 where they spent October 19th and 20th shooting location footage. Redlands was more than an hour from General Service Studios, but it was the perfect setting for what the producers needed to portray: a small town in general and a small *college* town in particular.

Perry visits the stately grounds of "Euclid College"—in reality the University of Redlands. The campus of the historic school is a producer's dream, with gorgeous grounds that lend an atmosphere of timelessness to the proceedings. We first see the tall, columned front of the University's Administration Building, which looks much the same now as it did then.

An establishing shot of a young man walking up the steps of the impressive building would later be re-used in another "Mason" outing, "The Case of the Prankish Professor." That episode, which also called for a college setting, aired only two years later and avoided location shooting. As a result, it looked studio-bound.

But the extensive location work on "Brazen Bequest" is a real treat for nostalgia fans. The episode takes advantage of almost all of the real sites of interest on the campus. At various times the background "stars" of the show are the

University quad, the Memorial Chapel, and the Greek Theater. The crew also filmed at the Redlands Bowl Stage.

The historic "La Posada Hotel" in downtown Redlands was featured on the show too.

At one point Hopper and Burr park their car around the corner from the Posada entrance, in front of "Willard's Dining Room and Cafeteria."

Paul and Perry at Willard's

Redlands doubled for the perfect American town back in December of 1961 when this episode was first shown. And in many ways, I guess it was.

Most of the Mason crew packed up and left Redlands late Friday, October 20th. It took about a week for the excitement to die down and then it was stirred up all over again when the "Brazen Bequest" aired for the first time on Saturday, December 2nd. Locals were thrilled about the national exposure.

There wasn't much not to like about Redlands in 1961— The University grounds looked lovely, La Posada was a famous hotel and Willard's, which had opened with great fanfare in October of 1958, looked like one of those perfect small town eateries of the day.

But, by 1965, Willard's had changed hands and by the early seventies a "downtown revitalization" plan was floated calling for the demolition of the La Posada. The hotel and its ground-level stores were demolished in the mid-seventies to make way for a huge mall. You can probably guess the rest of the story. After struggling for years, the mall closed in 2010 and stood vacant for years, a virtual ghost town.

Recently a new developer has taken over the property and old-timers in Redlands have been commenting on the long saga. Many wish they could go back to the "glory days" of the sixties and skip the days of demolition, financial trouble and political wrangling that took place in-between.

And deep down don't we all feel that way—no matter what decade we consider the "glory days?" I think many "Perry Mason" fans who've lived through the turbulent times of the more recent past can identify.

"Turbulent" is one thing, but "Nightmarish" is another. And the latter word is the only one that can be used to describe a deadly December 2015 attack that left 14 people dead in San Bernardino, California. Police said the massacre was carried out by a terrorist couple who lived in ... you guessed it ... Redlands. When they raided the home, authorities reported they found a "bomb factory" in the garage. What could be further from that ideal image of by-gone days that we still see in re-runs?

I know that Raymond Burr was right when he told me there were major changes going on in the world when he was shooting the original show. I also agree that all times present challenges and yesterday always tends to look better through the prism of memory. But to me, Redlands—both in real life and in "reel" life—best symbolizes the way this one TV show, "Perry Mason," served as a microcosm for events that were happening on a much larger scale in the country as a whole. And I think that explains why so many of us will always have such a feeling of nostalgia for the program.

THE CASE OF THE COUNSELOR'S COME BACK

If you want to know what Raymond Burr was really like, when it comes to the things that actually count about a person, look no further than his attitude toward everyday fans. When he was making the rounds to promote the "Perry Mason" TV movies, he came to see me early in the morning. It was an 8 o'clock appointment. Nobody else came in until later, so we walked through the outer office where there were lots of empty desks at that hour, and entered my office.

By the time we finished everybody else had arrived. It's pretty hard to hide Raymond Burr, so everyone was excited as we made our way through the outer room. And he went out of his way to stop at every desk, shake hands and say a few words to each person that wanted to speak with him. That's not the kind of thing that used to happen very often.

The other thing I remember thinking that day was that, here's this guy who has been a major celebrity for years, yet he remains humble despite his fame, which is not the case for many actors who achieve stardom. It seemed to me Burr genuinely enjoyed spending time with fans.

I spoke with him just before the launch of the "Mason" TV movies in the mid-eighties. At that point, the first one had been filmed and it was scheduled to air as a one-shot program. I asked him whether he would reprise the roll in additional shows, and he gave me that funny, sort of lop-sided smile he often used on the show when he was talking with "Della Street" or "Paul Drake."

"It all depends," he said, "on whether the public is willing to put up with me playing Perry Mason 27 years later."

Burr wasn't speaking with the fake self-effacement that some actors use to mask their hunger for applause. He seemed to be simply realistic and open to whatever happened. Raymond knew he was quite a bit older and quite a bit heavier and he realized tastes can change.

Fortunately for all of us, that first two-hour TV movie was a hit and more followed. And I think Burr genuinely enjoyed making the new shows.

"I always wanted to do a two-hour Perry Mason," he told me. "I had said that whenever someone got around to doing a two-hour show I'd do it. And that went on for a good many years. Then Fred Silverman came up with the idea. The Erle Stanley Gardner estate decided it was a good idea too, and I said 'Sure I'll do it.'" Silverman had been an executive at all three major networks before forming his own company.

"We had never done one during the time we were on the air with the hour show, and I always thought it really demanded two hours," Burr said.

Burr pushed for a longer format

I'm such a fan of the original series that I never saw any problem with the sixty minute length of the shows (although I do see major problems with the chopped up versions some cable outfits are showing these days to accommodate extra commercials. On occasion they eliminate material essential to the plot!) But Burr told me viewers of the hour shows were missing out whenever the programs were based on Erle Stanley Gardner novels and stories, which was frequently.

"We were never able to get all of Erle Stanley Gardner's clues and all the other good things he put in his books into one show," said Burr.

Comparing any of the novels with the TV versions makes this abundantly clear, especially when you consider the complicated plots of books like "The Case of the Crooked Candle," "The Case of the Empty Tin," "The Case of the Cautious Coquette," "The Case of the Foot-loose Doll," and "The Case of the Demure Defendant."

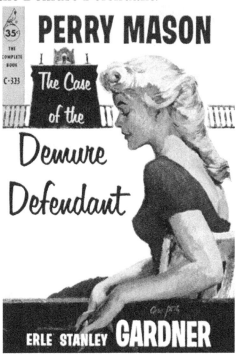

If you read the novels and then watch the television episodes, you realize how many characters had to be cut and how many chapters had to be abbreviated to squeeze the book into an hour show, which actually ran only 52 minutes.

In addition to the longer format, it was obvious Burr had other reasons to be so enthusiastic about the new project. He said he was especially impressed with Dean Hargrove, the TV mystery show veteran who was responsible for many of the scripts. After Burr finished shooting the first show, "Perry Mason Returns," he told me how much he liked the script, which had him defending Barbara Hale as Della Street.

"Dean wrote that script and he's Executive Producer along with Fred on the show. And I have to say it was a great experience. First of all we have this very good script and I think it makes for a very good show.

Burr took great interest in the scripts because he felt it would be harder to write for the newer shows.

"We had more material to work with at the beginning of the original "Perry Mason." We've gone through 30 years of material and writing on television since then."

"It's like music," he explained. "After a period of time, they say you can't get eight-bars that are completely new."

That may be true in music. But there's always something new in life. And Raymond Burr was lucky enough to find several new beginnings in his final years.

THE CASE OF THE FULFILLING FINALE

Although he may have, at times, invented some tall tales about his background, it seemed to me that Raymond Burr was fundamentally a pretty honest guy, especially about things that really mattered. I don't count the stories he made up about his private life because he had little choice. The truth would have put an end to his career before it even got started.

Burr at the beginning of his career

The one person I think Raymond Burr was occasionally (although quite unknowingly) dishonest with, was Raymond Burr!

For example, when we were talking about the rigors of doing a series, he told me, "After 'Perry Mason' I said I would never do another series, and then I did 'Ironside.'" The show ran for eight seasons.

He went on to explain how happy he was later, once he was free of the series grind and how it left him with time to do other things. This was all true as far as it went, but the message ... which I think he really believed ... was a bit misleading.

In his other long-running series, "Ironside"

Burr gave the impression that, had he not accepted "Ironside" in a moment of weakness, he would have spent the rest of his life in happy retirement. The evidence indicates that wasn't actually the case. If he really felt that way, why would the actor do the pilot for another proposed courtroom series called "Mallory" that aired in 1976? It was shown as a TV movie, but it failed to garner positive viewer reaction.

The show didn't catch on, despite the fact that it had an excellent cast. In addition to Burr, it featured Robert Loggia and Mark Hamill, who was only about a year away from his game-changing role as Luke Skywalker in "Star Wars."

Nevertheless, the fact that the pilot failed is not exactly the surprise of the century, since the lawyer Raymond plays in "Mallory" has none of Perry's almost super-human legal powers. Fans had come to expect a certain kind of lawyer from Burr and "Mallory" didn't fit the bill.

The script was also a far cry from the "Mason" series, with a plot that had Mallory defending a young prisoner accused of committing murder in connection with homosexual abuse in jail.

Raymond Burr as "Mallory" in 1976

Whatever "Mallory's" other problems, it didn't help any that Burr appeared throughout the show wearing the same curly hair-do he had when he appeared with William Lundigan in the low-budget pot-boiler, "Serpent of the Nile"

Burr & Lundigan in "Serpent of the Nile"

Burr followed "Mallory" almost right away with another show, "Kingston: Confidential," which also began as a TV pilot. But this one did get off the ground, even though it lasted for just 13 episodes because of low ratings.

The premise was an original one, if a little bit far-fetched. Burr played a media mogul who owned both newspapers and television stations, and yet still found time to do plenty of investigative work on the side. He was aided in his sleuthing by two young assistants—Pamela Hensley, who was later featured on the "Matt Houston" TV show, and Canadian actor Art Hindle, who went on to enjoy a prolific career in films.

"Kingston: Confidential" had a lot going for it, including an impressive list of guest stars such as Bradford Dillman, Dina Merrill, Diana Muldaur, Richard Mulligan, Frank Converse, Jack Carter, Henry Darrow, and Mariette Hartley.

Raymond with Mariette Hartley

Mariette is another one of my favorite people and I believe she and Raymond had much in common. Both were extremely easy to talk with and both faced very real challenges when they were younger. Raymond grew up without a father while Mariette had a father who, sadly, committed suicide.

A difficult childhood can frustrate a desire all of us have—the need to feel special, even if it's only to one person. More than a few actors got into the profession, in part, because it allowed them to feel special to many people. In other words, "The show must go on" not only for the audience, but for the actors as well.

So nobody should be too surprised that Raymond kept himself so busy for so long. I believe the truth is quite simple. Burr really enjoyed performing. While he tried to keep his private life private, from what I could see he really loved the fans. And, like many actors, while he might complain about the rigors of anchoring a series, he grew bored when he had too much time on his hands. He was often busy addressing lawyers groups and supporting all kinds of charities. And when he wasn't appearing on a series of his own, he was guest starring on someone else's show or doing a TV movie. It seemed as if he really needed to keep busy.

Burr guest starring on "Jack Benny"

I don't know if "workaholic" is the right word for it, but I think Raymond had to be active to feel really alive. When he was in "Perry Mason" he often spoke of how difficult it was to get any personal time, and he was absolutely right. But at that point in his life I don't think he would have been happy with too *much* time alone either.

Here was a guy who watched his parents separate when he was just a little kid. Having to say goodbye to his father at the age of five or six couldn't have been easy. And, as a young adult, scrambling to make his mark as an actor must have been difficult. In 1946, Burr was uncredited in the film "Without Reservations," and mentioned way down the credit list in "San Quentin."

With Lawrence Tierney & Carol Forman

I'm not sure he even realized it himself, but adjusting to the success of "Perry Mason" would take time. After struggling in the business for years, Raymond Burr finally found fame. He was assured of a weekly paycheck and quite a *large* paycheck at that. Despite a grueling schedule, he still squeezed in public appearances and charity work. And he would continue the heavy work load well beyond his "Perry Mason" days. Whether starting a new TV project or traveling to visit troops, he was constantly busy.

But later in life Raymond Burr seemed to find something that I think all of us search for—*balance*. Once the "Perry Mason" TV movies began, Burr could finally do what he loved to do at a reasonable pace. He enjoyed the work, especially the opportunity to act with Barbara Hale again and her son William Katt. But best of all, Burr told me, he finally had the time to pursue his dreams.

"I'm doing things now that I wanted to do for twenty years," he said. "I've always wanted to appear in London—in the West End—and now I've done a play there and I plan to do more." (Burr was talking about an appearance at the Prince of Wales Theatre in London, where he wrapped up a UK theatrical tour.)

Burr went on to say, "I have a tour of the United States planned too, and I've always wanted to tour Canada ... I was born there." The actor *did* get a chance to appear in Canada when he performed in the play "Underground" at the Royal Alexandra Theatre in Toronto.

Burr said, without the demands of a series, "I've gotten to the point where I can do all of the things I always wanted to do ... I've even got the farm in California." This was the same farm Raymond mentioned earlier, that eventually became the vineyards that he owned with Robert Benevides. He finally had time to enjoy the fruits of his labor *and* devote himself to the acting profession which he so loved. Burr kept it up almost until the end, when he lost his battle with cancer in 1993.

Raymond Burr was an amazing, complicated man who led an amazing, complicated life. He was around both before and well after the fifties and sixties, dealing with triumphs and troubles with equal grace. That alone should have answered the questions I had about any differences in decades.

Yet I still appreciate having had the opportunity to talk with him about whether the "good old days" were really all that good and the various other topics we discussed. It was Burr's compelling presence and personal charisma that defined Perry Mason, so much so that it is impossible today to imagine any other actor playing the role.

Raymond Burr was an intelligent, talented and generous man who worked hard at his craft and eventually found the life he was looking for. And, along the way, he left us with the legacy of America's favorite TV lawyer. What more could we ask for?

ABOUT THE AUTHOR

Brian McFadden is a veteran New York journalist and entertainment editor whose previous books include, "Republic Mysteries, The Serial Studio's Whodunits," and "Republic Horrors, The Serial Studio's Chillers." He is also the author of a popular book on the American-owned, British-based filmmaker "Amicus Productions," which has received widespread praise both in the US and the UK.

In addition to "Remembering Perry Mason with Raymond Burr," and other film and TV books, McFadden is the author of the groundbreaking music-reference classic, "Rock Rarities for a Song–A Guide to Budget LPs That Saved the Roots of Rock 'n' Roll." The author and his wife live in the Somerset Hills of New Jersey.

Note: The years that appear in connection with the films mentioned in this book generally refer to the release dates. The production dates often differ.

The illustrations in this reference/research work are used for historic and scholarly purposes under the "Fair Use Doctrine" of the US copyright law. While every effort has been made to provide proper acknowledgement where it is due, in the event any inadvertent omissions have occurred, we shall be pleased to correct them in future editions.

BAILEY BISHOPS

PRESS

Norman D. Hites, Rhode, Convent & Station

BY THE SAME AUTHOR:

The Only Two Books Exclusively Devoted to the Mystery and Horror Films of the Legendary Republic Studios!

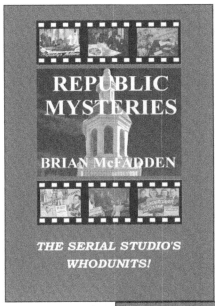

ALSO BY BRIAN MCFADDEN:

The First-Ever Guide to Budget LPs of the Fifties & Sixties
and the Rare Rock Treasures they contain!

"THE BUDGET RECORD BIBLE!"

— Frank Martin, member of "The Liverpools," "The Teachers," "The Scramblers" etc.

The Fantastic Story of Budget Record Labels and How They
Saved Precious Early Rock Classics by Otis Redding, Gene
Pitney, The Four Seasons, Lou Reed and so many others!

Remembering Perry Mason with Raymond Burr

Made in United States
North Haven, CT
23 December 2023

46537784R00063